150-CALORIE COCKTAILS

150-CALORIE COCKTAILS

ALL-NATURAL DRINKS AND SNACKS

Stephanie Banyas

Clarkson Potter/Publishers
New York

Copyright © 2015 by Clarkson Potter/Publishers

All rights reserved.
Published in the United States by Clarkson Potter/Publishers, an imprint of the
Crown Publishing Group, a division of Random House LLC, a Penguin Random
House Company, New York.
www.crownpublishing.com
www.clarksonpotter.com

CLARKSON POTTER is a trademark and POTTER with colophon is a registered
trademark of Random House LLC.

Library of Congress Cataloging-in-Publication Data
150-calorie cocktails. —First edition.
pages cm
Includes index.
1. Cocktails. 2. Low-calorie diet—Recipes.
I. Title: One hundred fifty–calorie cocktails.

TX951.A174 2014
641.87'4—dc23
2014040871

ISBN 978-0-8041-8621-6
eBook ISBN 978-0-8041-8622-3

Printed in China
Book design by La Tricia Watford
Cover design by Jessie Sayward Bright
Interior and cover photography by Tina Rupp

10 9 8 7 6 5 4 3 2 1

First Edition

CONTENTS

INTRODUCTION

Everyone loves a really fun cocktail! Cocktails can lift your spirits after a long workday, kick off an exciting vacation, and ring in the holidays like nothing else. But all those fun times can unfortunately pack on the calories before you know it. Even a well-crafted specialty cocktail is almost always filled with a lot of sugar and fat that can take all the joy out of cocktail hour. *150-Calorie Cocktails* has lots of low-calorie recipes, as well as clever tips and tricks that will let you once again enjoy fantastic mixed drinks without all the guilt. Plus, there are delicious snack recipes that are also amazingly low cal. Now you can put the "happy" back into Happy Hour!

SKINNY SIPPING & SMART SNACKING

A cocktail is defined as an alcoholic drink consisting of a spirit or several spirits mixed with other ingredients, such as fruit juice, lemonade, soda, and/or cream. The spirits themselves don't have all that many calories, depending on their proof, but boy, can those add-ins add up! Not to mention that even if you do choose a light beverage, most bar snacks are loaded with salt, fat, and calories. But never you fear! The recipes in this book are all you need to have a great time and not worry about your figure.

WHAT IS PROOF? Spirits are measured by proof. Alcohol proof is a measure of how much alcohol (ethanol) is contained in an alcoholic beverage. The amount of alcohol depends on how much was cooked off in the distilling process and how much water was added to bring the number down. The two most common proof amounts are 100 proof, which contains about 50% alcohol, and 80 proof, which contains about 40% alcohol. Why does 80 proof only contain 40% alcohol? In the United States, the proof of an alcoholic beverage is twice its alcohol content, expressed as percentage by volume at 60°F. So an 80 proof whiskey is 40% alcohol.

LET'S USE 80 PROOF VODKA AS AN EXAMPLE. On average, 80 proof vodka (40% alcohol) has 100 calories per shot (1½ ounces) and about 65 calories per ounce. The greater the vodka proof, the more calories per ounce. For an easy way to estimate the number of calories per ounce of vodka, subtract 15 from the vodka proof.

80 proof vodka / 80 − 15 = 65 calories per ounce

The number of ounces in a standard alcoholic drinks in the United States is 12 ounces for beer, 5 ounces for wine, and 1½ ounces for 80 proof liquor.

EASY TIPS FOR MAKING A LOW-CALORIE COCKTAIL

1 **Choose a lower-proof liquor.** All liquors with the same proof have roughly the same calories. In other words, 80 proof vodka has the same number of calories per ounce as 80 proof gin, bourbon, tequila, and so on. The lower the proof, the fewer calories a liquor has (and the less potent it will be). For example, 80 proof vodka has 65 calories an ounce; 100 proof vodka has about 85 calories an ounce. The recipes in this book use 80 proof because it's what you're most likely to find in your liquor store, and it seems to be the standard in upscale bars.

2 **Avoid prepared drink mixes,** which contain lots of corn syrup, not to mention artificial flavors and sweeteners. Make your own cocktails from scratch so you can control the calories and the ingredients.

3 **Skip the store-bought syrups**—such as sour mix–flavored syrups—and save calories by making your own flavored simple syrups (see page 11).

4 **Choose soda water or sparkling water over tonic water.** Tonic water looks innocent, but it actually has 90 calories per cup, unlike club soda and sparkling water, which are calorie free. Also, club soda and sparkling waters come in a variety of flavors these days, and all are natural and calorie free. Polar brand has an amazing variety of flavors that can be found throughout the country (www.polarbev.com).

5 **Dilute your wine with soda water or seltzer.** You'll stay hydrated, and a spritzer made with 3 ounces of wine and 2 ounces of soda water has only 60 calories. Add a few slices of fruit and you have a low-calorie sangria.

6 **Experiment with flavored liquors.** There is everything from citrus-, chile-, and berry-flavored vodkas and gins to chocolate-flavored tequila. And all of them contain the same number of calories as unflavored liquor: 96 calories per 80 proof shot (1½ ounces).

7 **Use sugar-free** sodas, fruit juices, lemonades, and iced teas.

THE LOW-CALORIE COCKTAIL PANTRY

Here is a list of things to have on hand, along with caloric information so you can create your own low-calorie libations.

LIQUOR AND WINE

RED WINE	5 ounces	Approx. 125 calories
SPARKLING WINE	5 ounces	Approx. 125 calories
WHITE WINE	5 ounces	Approx. 125 calories
GIN, 80 PROOF	1½ ounces	Approx. 96 calories
RUM, 80 PROOF	1½ ounces	Approx. 96 calories
TEQUILA, 80 PROOF	1½ ounces	Approx. 96 calories
WHISKEY, 80 PROOF	1½ ounces	Approx. 96 calories
VODKA, 80 PROOF	1½ ounces	Approx. 96 calories
LIGHT BEER	12 ounces	103–110 calories
REGULAR BEER	12 ounces	138 calories

MIXERS

COLA	12 ounces	140 calories
DIET SODA (ALL)	12 ounces	0 calories
GRAPEFRUIT JUICE	12 ounces	144 calories
LEMON-LIME SODA	12 ounces	140 calories
LIGHT ORANGE JUICE	12 ounces	75 calories
ORANGE JUICE	12 ounces	170 calories
PINEAPPLE JUICE	12 ounces	240 calories
LEMON JUICE	1 lemon	17 calories
LIME JUICE	1 lime	10 calories
APPLE CIDER	8 ounces	116 calories
COCONUT WATER	8 ounces	46 calories
COFFEE OR TEA	8 ounces	0 calories
CRANBERRY JUICE	8 ounces	140 calories
DIET LEMONADE (Newman's)	8 ounces	20 calories
LIGHT ORANGE JUICE	8 ounces	50 calories
LEMONADE (Newman's)	8 ounces	110 calories
TOMATO JUICE	8 ounces	40 calories

SWEETENERS

AGAVE 19–22 calories per teaspoon

CONFECTIONERS' SUGAR 10 calories per teaspoon

HONEY 22 calories per teaspoon

SIMPLE SYRUP 45 calories per tablespoon

SUGAR 15 calories per teaspoon

SUPERFINE SUGAR 15 calories per teaspoon

FUN ADDITIONS

COCOA POWDER, SWEETENED 35 calories per tablespoon

COCOA POWDER, UNSWEETENED 12 calories per tablespoon

FAT-FREE HALF-AND-HALF 20 calories per tablespoon

FRESH HERBS 0 calories

HERSHEY'S LIGHT CHOCOLATE SYRUP 22.5 calories per tablespoon

SKIM PLUS MILK 110 calories per 8 ounces

SPICES 0 calories

---

skim plus milk When shopping for milk to make these drinks, make sure you get Skim Plus brand milk. It's just as skinny as other milks but has the body and texture of the full-fat variety.

SIMPLE SYRUP

makes 1 cup

1 cup granulated sugar   **1 cup cold water**

In a small saucepan set over high heat, combine the sugar and water. Bring to a boil and cook until the sugar has completely dissolved, about 2 minutes.

Let cool to room temperature and transfer to a bowl. Cover and refrigerate until cold, at least 1 hour and up to 24 hours. The syrup will keep in an airtight container in the refrigerator for up to 1 month.

VARIATIONS

SOUR MIX SIMPLE SYRUP Add the grated zest of 1 orange, 1 lemon, and 1 lime. Store the syrup with the zest in the container.
CITRUS SIMPLE SYRUP Add 2 tablespoons grated zest of lemon, lime, orange, grapefruit, or tangerine, or a combination of any.
BERRY SIMPLE SYRUP Add 1 cup raspberries, blackberries, chopped strawberries, or blueberries.
CONCORD GRAPE SIMPLE SYRUP Add 1 cup Concord grapes and cook for 5 minutes.
MINT SIMPLE SYRUP Add ¼ cup packed fresh mint leaves.
SPICED SIMPLE SYRUP Add 2 cinnamon sticks, 1 star anise, 8 whole cloves, and 4 black peppercorns.
FRESH GINGER SIMPLE SYRUP Add ¼ cup peeled and chopped fresh ginger.
HONEY SIMPLE SYRUP Bring 1 cup honey and 1 cup water to a boil, let cool, and refrigerate. Add any of the above flavorings, if desired.

THE
CLASSICS

SHANDY

77 calories per serving

Popular in the United Kingdom, where it's also known as a Shandygaff, this cocktail is usually made of equal parts beer and carbonated lemonade. If you can't find sparkling lemonade in your grocery store, you can also use a lemon-lime soda, such as Sprite or Diet Sprite. It's really quite refreshing and fun! **Serves 3**

12 ounces very cold light beer, such as Bud Light

12 ounces very cold sparkling lemonade

Ice cubes

3 thin slices of lemon, for garnish

3 fresh mint sprigs, for garnish (optional)

In a pitcher, combine the beer and lemonade.

Fill 3 chilled tall glasses with ice cubes and divide the drink among the glasses. Garnish with a lemon slice and a fresh mint sprig, if desired, and serve.

VARIATIONS

BLOOD ORANGE SHANDY Substitute sparkling blood orange juice for the sparkling lemonade.

BEER MIMOSA Substitute orange juice for the sparkling lemonade.

EL LUCHADOR

102 calories per serving

It is said that this cocktail will give you the strength
of the famous Mexican wrestlers, the *luchadores*, whom the
drink is named after—or you can just kick back and
imbibe while watching them on TV. This cocktail is best
served in a chilled, frosty glass. **Serves 1**

4 ounces very cold Clamato juice

6 ounces very cold Corona Light

Juice of 1 lime

2 tablespoons fresh orange juice

Few dashes of Tabasco sauce or your favorite hot sauce

Pinch of ground cumin

Pinch of freshly ground black pepper

Pinch of kosher salt

Ice cubes (optional)

In a chilled glass, combine the Clamato, beer, lime and orange
juices, hot sauce, cumin, black pepper, and salt into the glass. Stir
well. Add ice cubes, if desired.

MICHELADA

64 calories per serving

This beer-based cocktail—always served in a salt-rimmed glass—is a Mexican classic that many believe to be a remedy for hangovers. Regardless, it is a perfect cocktail to sip by the pool or in front of the TV on game day! **Serves 2**

Kosher salt or sea salt

Juice of 4 limes (about 2 ounces), rinds reserved

Ice cubes

12 ounces very cold Corona Light

2 teaspoons Worcestershire sauce

4 dashes of hot sauce, or more if you like it spicier

2 pinches of freshly ground black pepper

Place enough salt in a wide, shallow dish to cover the bottom. Rub the rim of 2 rocks glasses with the lime rinds and dip the glasses into the salt. Fill the glasses with ice cubes and set aside.

In a small pitcher, combine the lime juice, beer, Worcestershire sauce, and hot sauce and stir well. Pour the drinks into the prepared glasses, top with a pinch of pepper, and serve.

VARIATION

MICHELADA WITH TEQUILA FLOATER Float 1 ounce of silver tequila on the top of the Michelada. (calories: 128)

GIN GIMLET

140 calories per serving

A 1928 description of the gimlet reads: "gin, a spot of lime, and soda." That means it's naturally low calorie! However, somewhere along the way, Rose's Lime Juice—a sweetened bottled lime juice that contains 10 calories per teaspoon—replaced fresh lime juice and increased the sweetness of this drink and also its calorie content. Fresh lime juice and simple syrup add a fresher, less sweet flavor to this "old school" libation and make it much more figure friendly. **Serves 1**

Ice cubes

1½ ounces best-quality gin

Finely grated zest and juice of ½ lime

1 tablespoon Simple Syrup or Citrus Simple Syrup (page 11)

Lime wedge, for garnish

Fill a cocktail shaker with ice cubes, and then add the gin, lime zest and juice, and simple syrup. Stir for 5 seconds, and then strain into a cocktail glass.

Squeeze the lime wedge into the glass and add the lime wedge to the glass, and serve.

VARIATION

VODKA OR RUM GIMLET Replace the 1½ ounces of gin with 1½ ounces of good-quality vodka or white rum.

MULLED RED WINE

127 calories per serving

What could be cozier than a toasty mug of mulled wine on a cold winter night? This classic cocktail has been warming people for centuries and is a sophisticated low-calorie alternative to creamy spiked coffees and hot chocolates. Plus, let's not overlook the heart-healthy benefits of red wine!

Serves 6

1 bottle fruity red wine, such as merlot

½ cup water

½ orange, thinly sliced

1 small lemon, halved and thinly sliced

1 pear, halved and thinly sliced

3 cinnamon sticks

2 star anise

4 whole cloves

In a medium nonreactive saucepan set over medium heat, combine the wine, water, orange slices, lemon slices, pear slices, cinnamon sticks, star anise, and cloves. Bring to a simmer and cook until fragrant, about 15 minutes. Remove the pan from the stove, cover, and let steep for 10 minutes. Serve in heatproof mugs or wine glasses.

MIMOSA

103 calories per serving

What would brunch be without the mimosa? Cutting back on the amount of orange juice and sparkling wine makes this version very calorie friendly. You can also use low-calorie orange juice to reduce the calories even more. **Serves 1**

2 ounces fresh orange juice

3 ounces sparkling wine

1 ounce orange-flavored club soda

1 strip of orange zest, for garnish

Put the orange juice in a chilled champagne flute and then add the sparkling wine and club soda. Garnish with the orange strip and serve.

WINE SPRITZER

100 calories per serving

It doesn't get much simpler, more low cal, or more refreshing than a wine spritzer. Funny how just a splash of something fizzy and some fruit can turn an ordinary glass of wine into a celebration! **Serves 1**

4 ounces white or red wine

2 ounces plain or flavored club soda or sparkling water

Fresh fruit (berries, grapes, lemon, and/or lime), for garnish

In a wine glass, combine the wine and soda. Garnish with fruit and serve.

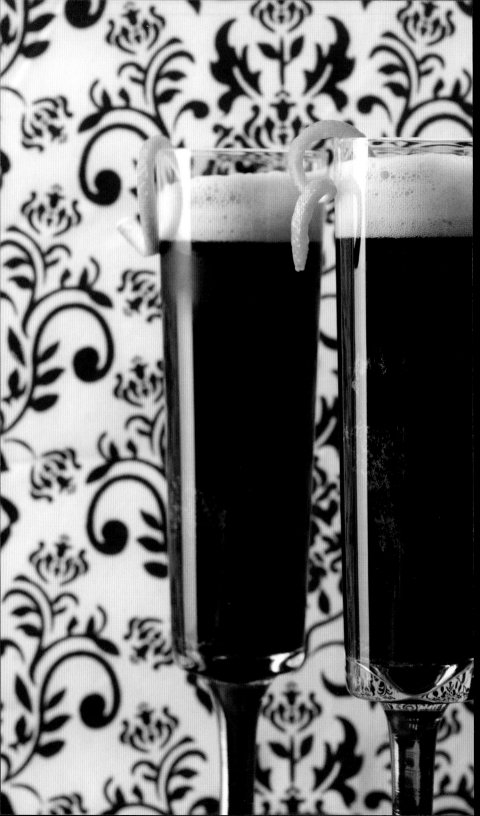

BLACK VELVET

113 calories per serving

According to the Guinness Storehouse, this cocktail was invented in 1861 at London's Brook's Club soon after the death of Prince Albert. In his grief, the club's steward declared that "even the champagne should be put into mourning," and he mixed it with the inky Guinness. Despite its dark color and full flavor, Guinness has far fewer calories than most beers, with 125 calories per 12 ounces. **Serves 1**

3 ounces cold Guinness stout

3 ounces cold sparkling wine

Orange twist, for garnish

Pour the stout into a chilled champagne flute, followed by the sparkling wine. Garnish with the orange twist and serve.

KIR SPRITZER

128 calories per serving

Kir is a classic French cocktail that's made with white wine and crème de cassis, a black currant liqueur. Its deep pinkish-red color is beautiful and so festive! **Serves 1**

3 ounces cold white wine

2 teaspoons crème de cassis

2 ounces raspberry or blackberry club soda

In a chilled champagne flute, combine the wine and crème de cassis. Top with the club soda and serve. **Serves 1**

VARIATIONS

KIR ROYALE Substitute champagne for white wine.

KIR PÊCHE Substitute champagne for white wine and peach liqueur for crème de cassis.

KIR IMPERIAL Substitute champagne for white wine and Chambord for crème de cassis.

WHITE WINE SANGRIA

104 calories per serving

Spanish-born sangria is a wonderfully refreshing fruity drink, but the combination of wine, brandy, triple sec, and fruit juice can add up to a calorie nightmare. Getting the fruity flavor from fruit alone, plus the addition of fruit-flavored club soda, makes it much more figure friendly. If you nibble on some of the fruit while drinking, it will add a few more healthy calories! *With fruit it's 137 calories!* **Serves 6**

1 bottle fruity dry white wine, such as sauvignon blanc

1 green apple, cored and thinly sliced

½ pint ripe fresh raspberries

½ orange, halved and thinly sliced

3-inch strip of orange zest

2-inch strip of lime zest

Splash of orange-flavored club soda

In a pitcher, combine the wine, apple slices, raspberries, orange slices, orange zest, and lime zest. Cover and refrigerate for at least 1 hour and up to 24 hours.

To serve, divide the sangria among 6 wine glasses and fill to the top with club soda.

VARIATION

RED WINE SANGRIA Substitute 5 ounces of the wine with a dry, fruity red wine, such as merlot, and blackberries for raspberries.

CLASSIC SAKETINI

135 calories per serving

This drink is essentially a Japanese martini. Sake (or saké) is an alcoholic beverage of that is made from fermented rice. It is sometimes called "rice wine," but the brewing process is more akin to beer making, where starch is converted to sugar during the fermentation process. It is relatively low in calories, coming in at 39 calories per ounce. **Serves 1**

1½ ounces gin

1 ounce sake

Ice cubes

2 thin slices cucumber, for garnish

1 fresh basil leaf, for garnish

In a cocktail shaker, combine the gin, sake, and ice cubes. Shake for 10 seconds.

Strain into a chilled martini glass, garnish with the cucumber slices and basil, and serve immediately.

VARIATION

VODKA-SAGE SAKETINI Substitute vodka for the gin and a sage leaf for the basil leaf.

CRANBERRY-GINGER SAKETINI

137 calories per serving

This cocktail is to the saketini what the Cosmopolitan is to the martini. **Serves 1**

1-inch piece fresh ginger, peeled and chopped

3 fresh mint leaves

1 teaspoon agave or Simple Syrup (page 11)

Ice cubes

1 ounce cold vodka or gin

1 tablespoon cold sake

1 ounce cranberry juice

Lime or orange twist, for garnish

Muddle the ginger, mint, and agave in the bottom of a cocktail shaker. Add the ice cubes, vodka, sake, and cranberry juice and shake for 10 seconds.

Strain into a chilled martini glass, garnish with a lime or orange twist, and serve.

SAKE COCKTAIL
117 calories per serving

Coconut water is credited with everything from boosting metabolism to replacing electrolytes after a hard workout. It also makes a healthy mixer for cocktails, giving great coconut flavor without fat or calories. **Serves 1**

3 ounces ice-cold coconut water

2 ounces ice-cold sake

Juice of ½ lime

1 teaspoon agave

Crushed ice

Lime wedge, for garnish

In a cocktail shaker, combine the coconut water, sake, lime juice, and agave, and stir well.

Fill a rocks glass with crushed ice and pour the drink over the ice. Garnish with the lime wedge and serve.

GIN MARTINI

129 calories per serving

James Bond prefers his martinis shaken, not stirred, and with vodka, not gin. Homer Simpson prefers his full of alcohol. Probably the most archetypal of all cocktails, the martini puts the "class" in classic. It is a very simple cocktail that contains just two ingredients: gin and dry vermouth. The less vermouth you put in the drink, the "drier" it is. Garnished with either of twist of lemon or lime or a few pitted green Spanish olives (which are about 10 calories each), it is a naturally low-calorie choice—and you look very cool drinking it. **Serves 1**

1½ ounces dry gin

½ ounce dry vermouth

1 dash of orange bitters
(optional)

Ice cubes

1 strip of lemon zest

In a cocktail shaker, combine the gin, vermouth, and bitters, if using. Fill the shaker with ice cubes and stir well, and then strain into a chilled cocktail glass. To serve, twist the lemon zest over the drink and use as a garnish.

VARIATIONS

VODKA MARTINI Substitute vodka for the gin and omit the bitters.
DIRTY VODKA MARTINI Stir 1 tablespoon of the briny liquid of green olives into the drink and garnish with 2 olives. (calories: 149)

GIN FIZZ

140 calories per serving

This is the cooler cousin of the gin and tonic. With lots of lemon and lime flavor from the citrus zest and sweetness from the addition of simple syrup, you can definitely think of it as Sprite for adults. **Serves 1**

1½ ounces gin

¼ teaspoon finely grated lemon zest

¼ teaspoon finely grated lime zest

1 tablespoon fresh lemon juice

1 tablespoon fresh lime juice

2 teaspoons Simple Syrup (page 11)

Crushed ice

Lemon-lime club soda

Lemon and or lime wedge, for garnish

In a cocktail shaker, combine the gin, lemon and lime zests, lemon and lime juices, and simple syrup. Fill the shaker with ice cubes and shake for 10 seconds.

Strain the drink into a rocks glass filled with ice and add a few splashes of club soda. Garnish with the lemon wedge and serve.

GIN & TONIC

96 calories per serving

Because of its historical connection with warm climates, gin and tonic is a popular cocktail during the warmer months. Nothing is better on a hot summer day than this refreshing libation served on the rocks with a wedge of lime. Don't let tonic water fool you—it actually contains about 10 calories an ounce. This version uses club soda, which contains no calories and tastes practically the same. Try using lime-flavored club soda for additional lime flavor with no additional calories. **Serves 1**

Ice cubes

1½ ounces gin

3 ounces cold club soda, plain or lime flavored

Lime wedge

Fill a glass with ice cubes and add the gin and soda. Squeeze the lime wedge into the drink, add the wedge to the glass, and serve.

TOM COLLINS

148 calories per serving

The best way to describe a Tom Collins is that it's sparkling lemonade for adults. This classic gin cocktail has been around for more than a century and has recently seen a resurgence in popularity thanks to the AMC show *Mad Men*. **Serves 1**

1½ ounces gin

1 ounce fresh lemon juice

2 teaspoons Simple Syrup (page 11)

Ice cubes

3 ounces lemon club soda

1 thin slice orange, for garnish

1 maraschino cherry, for garnish

In a Collins glass, combine the gin, lemon juice, and simple syrup.

Fill the glass to the top with ice cubes and add the soda. Garnish with the orange slice and cherry and serve.

GIN RICKEY

111 calories per serving

Similar to a gin and tonic but with much more tart lime flavor, this drink was originally made with bourbon. However, it only became widely popular once it was made with gin instead.

Serves 1

Ice cubes

1¼ ounces gin

Juice of 1 lime

1 teaspoon agave or Simple Syrup (page 11)

2 ounces lime-flavored club soda

In a rocks glass filled with ice cubes, combine the gin, lime juice, and agave. Add the club soda and serve.

VARIATION

CHERRY-LIME GIN RICKEY Add 1 teaspoon of maraschino cherry juice along with the gin, lime juice, and agave. Garnish with a maraschino cherry. (calories: 121)

FRENCH 75

136 calories per serving

The French 75 is basically a Tom Collins with champagne added. **Serves 1**

1 ounce gin

1 ounce fresh lemon juice

1 teaspoon Simple Syrup (page 11)

2 ounces cold sparkling wine or champagne

Lemon twist, for garnish

Pour the gin, lemon juice, and simple syrup into a chilled champagne flute. Add the sparkling wine, garnish with the lemon twist, and serve.

DAISY

116 calories per serving

This rendition of the classic long cocktail is slimmed and trimmed and oh-so-delicious. The alcohol has been scaled back, and the homemade red-berry simple syrup has fewer calories but still lots of flavor. **Serves 1**

1 ounce gin

1 tablespoon Berry Simple Syrup (page 11)

1 tablespoon fresh lemon juice

Crushed ice

Raspberry-flavored club soda

Orange or lemon slice, for garnish

Stir together the gin, simple syrup, and lemon juice in a tall cocktail glass.

Add crushed ice and fill to the top with club soda. Garnish with the orange slice and serve.

SALTY DOG

120 calories per serving

This classic cocktail is the salt-inflected version of another classic, the Greyhound. They're made the same way, only this one is made with gin instead of vodka, and the rim of the glass gets a sweet/salty dusting. **Serves 1**

1 teaspoon kosher salt

¼ teaspoon sugar

1 lime wedge

Ice cubes

2 ounces pink or yellow grapefruit juice

1½ ounces gin

Grapefruit-flavored club soda or Squirt (or another calorie-free grapefruit soda)

Combine the salt and sugar on a small plate. Rub the rim of a tall glass with the lime wedge and dip the rim of the glass in the salt mixture.

Fill the glass with ice cubes, then add the grapefruit juice and gin and fill to the top with the club soda. Garnish with the same lime wedge you used to rim the glass and serve.

VARIATION

GREYHOUND Substitute vodka for the gin and serve in an unsalted glass.

COSMOPOLITAN

113 calories per serving

There is a reason that Carrie and her friends loved this drink . . . it's naturally low in calories, pink, and delicious! Use a cranberry- or orange-flavored vodka to cut back on the cranberry juice, and use orange-flavored club soda to save on the very caloric orange liqueur (188 calories per 1½ ounces!).

Serves 1

1½ ounces cranberry- or orange-flavored vodka

1 ounce cranberry juice

Ice cubes

2 ounces orange-flavored club soda

Lime wedge

Orange twist, for garnish

In a cocktail shaker, combine the vodka and juice, fill with ice cubes, and shake for 10 seconds.

Strain into a martini glass, add the club soda, and squeeze the lime wedge into the drink. Garnish with the orange twist and serve.

LEMON DROP

103 calories per serving

Rumor has it that this drink was created sometime in the 1970s at a San Francisco bar called Henry Africa's, and that their goal was to popularize so-called girly drinks. Well, everyone is glad they did, because this drink is the perfect combination of sweet and sour, and, with a few tweaks, it's very low cal. Using lemon-flavored vodka makes all the difference in the cocktail—the lemon flavor is off the charts!

Serves 1

Juice of 1 lemon

1½ teaspoons superfine
sugar

Ice cubes

1½ ounces very cold
lemon-flavored vodka

1 tablespoon fresh orange
juice

Splash of lemon- or
orange-flavored club soda
(optional)

Put half the lemon juice onto a small plate. Put ½ teaspoon of the sugar onto another small plate to coat the bottom. Dip the rim of a martini glass in the lemon juice and then run the rim around in the sugar. Put the glass in the refrigerator for at least 5 minutes.

In a cocktail shaker filled with ice cubes, combine the remaining lemon juice, the remaining 1 teaspoon of sugar, the vodka, and the orange juice. Shake for 20 seconds.

Remove the prepared glass from the refrigerator, strain the drink into the glass, and serve.

SEA BREEZE

130 calories per serving

Since its creation in 1920, this Cape Cod favorite has gone through many incarnations. Today the Sea Breeze contains vodka, cranberry juice, and grapefruit juice. The addition of two sugary fruit juices jacks up the calorie content of this seemingly simple summer classic, so our version contains grapefruit vodka, grapefruit-flavored club soda, and a touch of cranberry juice. **Serves 1**

Ice cubes

1½ ounces Ruby Red Grapefruit Vodka

2 ounces cranberry juice

2 ounces grapefruit- or cranberry-flavored or plain club soda

Fill a rocks glass with ice cubes and add the vodka and cranberry juice.

Fill to the top with club soda and serve.

DARK 'N STORMY

132 calories per serving

The name of this cocktail is trademarked by Gosling's Export Limited of Bermuda, makers of Gosling's Black Seal Rum and Gosling's Stormy Ginger Beer. The Dark 'n Stormy is the company's signature drink and consists of their rum and ginger beer served over ice, optionally accompanied by a slice of lime. The original recipe is served in a Collins glass, with more rum and ginger beer than this recipe, which is trimmed down to make it figure friendly. **Serves 1**

1½ ounces Gosling's Black Seal Rum

Ice cubes

3 ounces ginger beer

Lime wedge

Pour the rum into a rocks glass filled with ice cubes and add the ginger beer.

Squeeze the lime wedge into the drink, add the wedge to the glass, and serve.

BLOODY MARY

129 calories per serving

What other drink can claim to be a hangover cure and be a nutritious brunch cocktail at the same time? A Bloody Mary is full of flavor, and the good news is that it is naturally low in calories. Make it as spicy or as mild as you like. **Serves 1**

5 ounces very cold tomato juice

1½ ounces vodka

Juice of ½ lime

Juice of ½ lemon

2 teaspoons prepared horseradish

2 dashes of Worcestershire sauce

2 dashes of Tabasco sauce

Pinch of celery salt

Pinch of smoked paprika or regular paprika

Pinch of freshly ground black pepper

Ice cubes

1 small celery stalk, for garnish

1 lime wedge, for garnish

Combine the tomato juice, vodka, lime and lemon juices, horseradish, Worcestershire sauce, Tabasco sauce, celery salt, paprika, and black pepper in a tall glass.

Add ice, garnish with the celery stalk and lime wedge, and serve.

VARIATION

BLOODY CAESAR Substitute 5 ounces of Clamato juice for the tomato juice. (calories: 137)

MOSCOW MULE

142 calories per serving

This classic cocktail is traditionally served in a copper mug, though a chilled highball glass will do just fine. Ginger beer isn't alcoholic at all. It's similar to ginger ale but with a more pronounced ginger flavor. If you can't find it, you can use ginger ale, which has only 1 calorie more per ounce, or use diet ginger ale if you want to save even more calories.

Serves 1

Ice cubes

1½ ounces vodka

3 ounces ginger beer or
   ginger ale

Juice of 1 lime

Lime wedge, for garnish

In a rocks glass filled with ice cubes, combine the vodka, ginger beer, and lime juice. Garnish with the lime wedge and serve.

RUM & COKE

148 calories per serving
(with Diet Coke: 96 calories)

This quintessential college cocktail is still a winner, especially on a hot summer day while sitting at the pool. You can lower the calories even more by using Diet Coke, if that is your thing, or add a kick by replacing regular dark rum with spiced rum. **Serves 1**

Ice cubes

1½ ounces dark rum or spiced rum

4 ounces Coke or Diet Coke

Lime wedge, for garnish

Fill a short tumbler with ice cubes, then add the rum and Coke. Stir to combine. Garnish with the lime wedge and serve.

VARIATION

CUBA LIBRE This Cuban cousin contains white rum, Coke, and a squeeze of lime juice served over ice cubes in a highball glass.

THE PALOMA

101 calories per serving

This classic Mexican cocktail, made with lime juice, tequila, and grapefruit-flavored soda, is refreshing, tasty, and naturally low calorie. **Serves 1**

Ice cubes

1½ ounces tequila

Juice of ½ lime

5 ounces grapefruit-flavored soda (such as Fresca) or grapefruit-flavored club soda

Lime wedge, for garnish

In a tall glass filled with ice cubes, combine the tequila, lime juice, and soda. Garnish with the lime wedge and serve.

MOJITO

136 calories per serving

This lime- and mint-flavored cocktail is relatively low in alcohol content but high in calories because of the large amount of sugar or cane syrup typically used to prepare it. By simply cutting back on the sugar you can still enjoy all that is wonderful about this refreshing Cuban-born drink. **Serves 1**

4 fresh mint leaves, plus a sprig for garnish

2 teaspoons Simple Syrup, Mint Simple Syrup, or lime-flavored Simple Syrup (page 11)

1 teaspoon finely grated lime zest

Juice of 1 lime

1½ ounces white rum

Crushed ice

Lime-flavored club soda

Muddle the mint leaves, simple syrup, lime zest, and lime juice in the bottom of a highball glass. Add the rum and a handful of crushed ice.

Fill the glass with the club soda, garnish with the mint sprig, and serve.

VARIATION

COCO MOJITO Substitute coconut rum for the white rum.

TEQUILA & SODA

96 calories per serving

This simple, refreshing, and naturally low-calorie cocktail contains only two ingredients, tequila and soda. **Serves 1**

Ice cubes

1½ ounces good-quality silver or gold tequila

4 ounces plain or flavored club soda (orange or lime or a combination of both)

Lime wedge or twist, for garnish

In a rocks glass filled with ice cubes, stir together the tequila and club soda. Garnish with the lime wedge and serve.

VARIATION

SPICED TEQUILA AND SODA Add 2 teaspoons of Spiced Simple Syrup (page 11) for a modern twist (calories: 126).

MARGARITA

115 calories per serving

Margaritas look innocent enough, but the combination of tequila, sour mix, and orange liqueur can add up to more than 270 calories when ordered at your favorite bar. By getting rid of the sour mix and orange liqueur and substituting fresh lime, fresh orange juice, and club soda, you get the same amazing flavor and save more than 150 calories per glass! **Serves 1**

1½ ounces silver tequila	**Ice cubes**
1 tablespoon fresh orange juice	**Orange- or lime-flavored club soda**
1 tablespoon fresh lime juice	**Lime or orange twist, for garnish**

Combine the tequila and orange and lime juices in a highball glass. Fill the glass with ice cubes and top with club soda.

To serve, run the lime twist around the rim and add to the drink as a garnish.

VARIATION

SALTED MARGARITA Combine 1 tablespoon freshly squeezed lime juice and 1 tablespoon freshly squeezed orange juice on a small plate. Evenly spread 1 teaspoon kosher salt on another flat plate. Dip the rim in the juice and then in the salt. Make the Margarita as directed.

DAIQUIRI

138 calories per serving

This cocktail was invented in the village of Daiquiri in Cuba more than one hundred years ago. Another naturally low-calorie drink, it never fails to please. **Serves 1**

Ice cubes

1¼ ounces light rum

Juice of 1 lime

1 teaspoon finely grated lime zest

1 tablespoon Simple Syrup (page 11)

Splash of lime-flavored club soda

Lime slice, for garnish

Fill a cocktail shaker with ice. Add the rum, lime juice, lime zest, and simple syrup and shake for 10 seconds.

Strain into a chilled martini glass and fill to the top with the club soda. Garnish with the lime slice and serve.

HEMINGWAY
DAIQUIRI

143 calories per serving

It is said that the Hemingway Daiquiri was invented for Ernest Hemingway in the El Floradita Bar in Havana, Cuba, and that he loved it so much that he would always order a double. The original includes a cherry liqueur that has quite a few calories and isn't easy to find, but adding a few teaspoons of maraschino cherry juice will do the trick, giving this daiquiri a lovely pink hue. **Serves 1**

Ice cubes

1¼ ounces light rum

¼ cup grapefruit juice

Juice of 1 lime

2 teaspoons maraschino cherry juice

1 maraschino cherry, for garnish

Lime wheel, for garnish

Fill a cocktail shaker with ice cubes.

Add the rum, grapefruit juice, lime juice, and maraschino cherry juice and shake for 10 seconds.

To serve, strain into a rocks glass and garnish with the cherry and the lime wheel.

TEQUILA SUNRISE

142 calories per serving

Mexico is vibrant! Just walk down the streets and you will
find that everywhere bright colors reach out and grab you.
This drink is like Mexico in a glass: festive, colorful, and fun!
Grenadine adds great color in addition to a tart cherry flavor.

Serves 1

1 ounce silver tequila

4 ounces fresh orange juice

½ ounce fresh lime juice

Ice cubes

**Splash of orange-flavored
club soda**

1 teaspoon grenadine

**Half an orange slice, for
garnish (optional)**

Combine the tequila and the orange and lime juices in a tall glass.
Fill with ice and top with a splash of club soda.

Float the grenadine on top (it will sink and then come back up to
the top, creating a sunrise effect). Garnish with the orange slice, if
desired, and serve.

JACK & COKE

142 calories per serving

Also known as JD and Coke, it doesn't get much simpler than this cocktail. Use Diet Coke and you have the perfect under-100-calorie cocktail. **Serves 1**

Ice cubes

1½ ounces Jack Daniel's

5 ounces Coke or Diet Coke

Lemon or lime wedge, for garnish

In a rocks glass or Collins glass filled with ice cubes, combine the Jack Daniel's and Coke. Garnish with the lemon wedge and serve.

MINT JULEP

144 calories per serving

The Run for the Roses takes place in Lexington on the first Saturday of May with the first stretch of the Triple Crown, the Kentucky Derby. In addition to lots of great southern food, the cocktail of the day is the mint julep. A classic julep weighs in at only about 165 calories, so by just cutting back on the sugar, you can enjoy this version for about 144 calories.

Serves 1

1 tablespoon Mint Simple Syrup (page 11)

1½ ounces bourbon

Crushed ice

Splash of club soda

1 fresh mint sprig, for garnish

Combine the simple syrup and bourbon in a mint julep cup or a rocks glass.

Fill to the rim with crushed ice and add a splash of club soda. Garnish with the mint sprig and serve.

VARIATION

BLACKBERRY MINT JULEP Muddle the mint syrup and 3 blackberries in the bottom of the glass, add the bourbon, crushed ice, and club soda, and garnish with a mint sprig. (calories: 150)

CIDERHOUSE

149 calories per serving

This cocktail is classically made with bourbon and cider syrup, a syrup made from boiled-down apple cider. Cider syrup can be found online at www.woodscidermill.com, but you can also get the same flavor by adding a splash of regular apple cider and a drizzle of maple syrup for a really lovely cocktail made for sipping—and that's only 145 calories.

Serves 1

1½ ounces bourbon

1 ounce cider syrup

Ice cubes

1 strip of lemon zest, for garnish

Stir together the bourbon and the cider syrup in the bottom of a rocks glass.

Add ice cubes, garnish with the lemon zest, and serve.

WHISKEY SOUR

141 calories per serving

This drink often gets a bad rap, most likely because of the bottom-shelf whiskey and the sickeningly sweet sour mix that many bars make it with. By simply using a good-quality whiskey or bourbon and homemade citrusy sour mix, this nineteenth-century cocktail is officially introduced to the twenty-first century. **Serves 1**

1½ ounces whiskey or bourbon

1 tablespoon Sour Mix Simple Syrup (page 11)

Ice cubes

Splash of orange-flavored club soda

Orange slice, for garnish

Maraschino cherry, for garnish

In a cocktail shaker, combine the whiskey and simple syrup with a few ice cubes. Shake for 10 seconds and pour into a rocks glass filled with ice cubes.

Top off with a splash of club soda, garnish with the orange slice and maraschino cherry, and serve.

OLD FASHIONED

134 calories per serving

Purists will tell you that a true Old Fashioned consists of nothing more than sugar, whiskey, bitters, and possibly a splash of water and a twist of orange. That definitely hits low on calorie count, but this colorful version is definitely worth trying. The addition of lemon, lime, and a maraschino cherry adds minimal calories, so go ahead and be modern! **Serves 1**

1 orange slice

1 lemon slice

1 lime slice

1 maraschino cherry

1 teaspoon sugar

Splash of cold water

3 dashes orange or regular Angostura bitters

1½ ounces rye or bourbon whiskey

Ice cubes

Splash of plain or orange-flavored club soda

Muddle the orange, lemon, and lime slices, maraschino cherry, sugar, and water in the bottom of a rocks glass. Stir in the bitters and whiskey.

Add ice cubes, a few splashes of club soda to taste, and serve.

GIRLY
COCKTAILS

WATERMELON MARTINI

145 calories per serving

Beautiful to look at and refreshing to drink, this martini may not be masculine enough for James Bond, but it's fantastic. The lime juice cuts the sweetness just a bit and adds a slight tang. **Serves 1**

Ice cubes

1½ ounces vodka

3 ounces fresh watermelon juice, homemade (recipe follows) or store bought

Juice of ½ lime

Thin slice of watermelon, for garnish

In a cocktail shaker filled with ice cubes, combine the vodka, watermelon juice, and lime juice. Shake for 10 seconds and strain into a martini glass. Garnish with the slice of watermelon and serve.

HOMEMADE FRESH WATERMELON JUICE

For 3 ounces of juice, start with ½ pound peeled, seeded, and chopped watermelon. Place it in a blender and blend until smooth. Strain through a strainer into a bowl. It will keep in an airtight container in the refrigerator for up to 2 days.

FIRE & ICE

135 calories per serving

If you like the combination of spicy and sweet, then you will love this cocktail. If you can't find pepper-infused vodka or tequila, just muddle half a jalapeño or serrano chile with the cucumber. **Serves 1**

1-inch piece of cucumber, peeled and chopped

2 teaspoons Simple Syrup (page 11)

Juice of ½ lime

Juice of ¼ lemon

1½ ounces jalapeño-flavored tequila or pepper-infused vodka

Ice cubes

Splash of lime-flavored club soda

Muddle the cucumber and simple syrup in the bottom of a cocktail shaker. Add the lime and lemon juices and the tequila and shake for 10 seconds.

Pour into a rocks glass filled with ice cubes, add a splash of club soda, and serve.

CONCORD GRAPE "SODA"

116 calories per serving

Making your own Concord grape simple syrup is the key to incredibly natural grape flavor in this beautifully hued cocktail. If you really want to be fancy, serve in a champagne flute and add a splash of sparkling wine (at only 25 calories an ounce). Freeze a few extra Concord grapes and add them to the cocktail in place of ice cubes. **Serves 1**

1 ounce gin

1 tablespoon Concord Grape Simple Syrup (page 11)

1 lime wedge

Crushed ice

3 ounces club soda or champagne

5 Concord grapes, frozen (optional)

Mix together the gin and grape syrup in a rocks glass.

Squeeze the lime and add to the glass. Add crushed ice and fill to top with the soda. Garnish with the frozen grapes, if desired, and serve.

VARIATION

VODKA GRAPE "SODA" Substitute vodka for the gin.

THE HONEY BEE

139 Calories

When I think of manly drinks, I think whiskey, straight up or with a drop of water. To make whiskey more palatable to feminine tastes, soften it with a touch of sweetness by adding honey and apple cider, as well as a bit of freshness with lemon juice. This cocktail is so good that the men may ask you to prepare one for them, too. **Serves 1**

1½ ounces whiskey

2 ounces apple cider

1 teaspoon honey

Juice of ½ lemon

Ice cubes

Splash of lemon-flavored seltzer or club soda

Lemon wedge, for garnish

In a cocktail shaker, combine the whiskey, apple cider, honey, lemon juice, and a few ice cubes and shake for 10 seconds.

Strain into a rocks glass filled with ice cubes and top with seltzer. Garnish with the lemon wedge and serve.

CHOCOLATE MARTINI

148 calories per serving

This is a perfect cocktail to serve to chocolate lovers or as an aperitif before a romantic meal with your significant other.

Serves 1

1½ ounces vodka

½ ounce chocolate liqueur (crème de cacao), such as Godiva

Ice cubes

½ teaspoon finely grated bittersweet chocolate, for garnish

In a cocktail shaker, combine the vodka, chocolate liqueur, and ice cubes and shake for 20 seconds.

Strain into a martini glass, garnish with the grated chocolate, and serve.

VARIATIONS

MOCHA MARTINI Substitute coffee-flavored vodka for regular vodka and garnish with a chocolate-covered espresso bean instead of the grated chocolate.

CHOCOLATE-COVERED ORANGE MARTINI Substitute orange-flavored vodka for regular vodka and garnish with grated chocolate and finely grated orange zest.

RUBY RED GRAPEFRUIT–LAVENDER GIN SODA

109 calories per serving

This easy-to-drink beverage is like a lemonade with a floral twist and a kick. Its pink hue and sparkle make it pretty and girly. **Serves 8**

½ cup sugar

1 cup water

1 small Ruby Red grapefruit, coarsely chopped

6 lavender flowers

8 ounces gin

1 quart grapefruit-flavored sparkling water or club soda

Ice cubes

8 slices Ruby Red grapefruit, for garnish

8 fresh mint sprigs, for garnish

In a medium saucepan combine the sugar, water, grapefruit, and lavender and bring to a boil over high heat. Reduce the heat to low and cook until the grapefruit is soft, about 10 minutes. Remove the pan from the heat and let cool to room temperature. Strain the syrup into a small pitcher or bowl, cover, and refrigerate until cold, about 1 hour and up to 24 hours.

Put the syrup into a pitcher and stir in the gin and sparkling water. Serve in tall glasses filled with ice cubes, each garnished with a grapefruit slice and a sprig of mint.

HIBISCUS SANGRIA

127 calories per serving

This hot-pink punch—which gets its lovely hue from the bright-magenta leaves of the hibiscus flower—will steal the show at your next celebration or brunch. Hibiscus tea has a tart cranberry-like flavor. You may find it in your grocery store's tea aisle under the name Red Zinger. **Serves 8**

2 cups water

3 hibiscus tea bags

1 tablespoon sugar

1 bottle cold fruity white wine, such as sauvignon blanc

4 ounces gin or vodka

1 cup Ruby Red grapefruit juice

1 orange, halved and thinly sliced

1 cup fresh raspberries

1 small Gala apple, cored, halved, and thinly sliced

In a small pot, bring 2 cups of water to a boil. Add the tea bags and sugar and let steep for 5 minutes. Discard the tea bags and let the tea cool to room temperature.

Transfer the cooled tea to a pitcher and add the wine, gin, grapefruit juice, orange slices, raspberries, and apple slices. Cover and refrigerate for at least 4 hours and up to 8 hours before serving.

Divide the drink among 8 wine glasses, making sure to get a little fruit in each, and serve.

FROZEN LIMEADE
MARGARITA
144 calories per serving

Pale-green, cool, refreshing, tangy limeade is a fantastic drink for a hot summer day. Turn it into an adult slushy with the addition of ice cubes and tequila! **Serves 10**

1 12-ounce can of good-quality frozen limeade (such as Newman's Own), partially thawed

4 cups ice cubes

10 ounces silver tequila or lime-flavored tequila

Finely grated zest of 2 limes

1 cup lime-flavored club soda

1 large orange, cut into 10 wedges

In a blender, combine the limeade, ice cubes, tequila, lime zest, and club soda and blend until smooth.

Divide among 10 glasses, squeeze an orange wedge over the top of each, and serve.

VARIATION

MINTED FROZEN LIMEADE MARGARITA Substitute white rum for the tequila, 12 fresh mint leaves for the lime zest, and lime wedges for the orange wedges.

POMEGRANATE SANGRIA GRANITA

117 calories per serving

Just when you thought sangria couldn't be more refreshing, here it is in an icy iteration. Basically a Spanish-style snow cone, it's oh-so-craveable on hot summer days! **Serves 6**

- **1 cup very cold 100% bottled pomegranate juice**
- **3 tablespoons Simple Syrup (page 11)**
- **2 teaspoons finely grated orange zest**
- **1 teaspoon finely grated lemon zest**
- **2 cups very cold fruity red wine, such as merlot**
- **Pomegranate seeds, for garnish (optional)**

In a medium bowl, combine the pomegranate juice, simple syrup, orange and lemon zests, and wine. Pour the mixture into a 10-inch shallow baking dish. Cover and freeze for about 30 minutes. Scrape the mixture with a fork and freeze for another 30 minutes. Repeat until the sangria is completely frozen, about 5 hours.

Remove the mixture from the freezer and scrape with a fork until the entire mixture is fluffy.

Serve in cups with spoons and garnish with a sprinkling of pomegranate seeds, if desired.

PEAR-SAGE
WINE COOLERS
140 calories per serving

These are not only low-calorie, refreshing cocktails but are also beautiful to look at. The combinations of fruits and herbs are endless, too. Create seasonal flavors using the freshest ingredients you can find. **Serves 7**

½ cup sugar

1 cup water

1 Bartlett pear, halved, cored, and thinly sliced

6 fresh sage leaves

1 bottle cold fruity white wine, such as sauvignon blanc

Cold club soda

In a medium nonreactive pan, combine the sugar and water and bring to a boil over high heat. Cook until the sugar has dissolved and the mixture begins to reduce slightly, about 5 minutes.

Add the pear slices and sage leaves, remove the pan from the heat, cover, and let steep until cooled to room temperature, about 30 minutes. Refrigerate for at least 1 hour and up to 24 hours.

Using a slotted spoon, divide the pear slices among 7 wine glasses and add 2 teaspoons of the syrup.

Fill each glass with 3½ ounces of wine, top off with a splash of club soda, and serve.

VARIATIONS

PEACH-BASIL WINE COOLER Substitute 1 halved, pitted, and thinly sliced peach for the pear and 6 fresh basil leaves for the sage.

STRAWBERRY-ROSEMARY WINE COOLER Substitute 7 quartered strawberries for the pear and 2 sprigs of fresh rosemary for the sage.

BLACKBERRY-THYME WINE COOLER Substitute 14 halved blackberries for the pear and 3 sprigs of fresh thyme for the sage.

BLACK RUSSIAN GRANITA

90 calories per serving

A Black Russian cocktail is simply equal parts of coffee
liqueur and vodka. This drink first appeared in 1949, at the
Hotel Metropole in Brussels, and owes its name to the use of
vodka, a typical Russian spirit, and the blackness of the coffee
liqueur. Our frozen version is the perfect pick-me-up on a
hot summer day or a perfect "cocktail" to serve at brunch.

Serves 6

**2 cups cold espresso or
strong coffee**

**¼ cup Simple Syrup
(page 11)**

4 ounces vanilla vodka

**2 ounces Kahlua or other
coffee liqueur**

**½ teaspoon finely grated
orange zest**

In a medium bowl, stir together the espresso, simple syrup, vodka,
Kahlua, and orange zest. Pour the mixture into a 10-inch baking
dish. Cover and freeze for about 45 minutes. Scrape with a fork
and freeze for another 45 minutes. Repeat until the mixture is
completely frozen, about 5 hours.

Remove the mixture from the freezer and scrape with a fork until
the entire mixture is fluffy. Serve in coffee cups with spoons.

BIRTHDAY CAKE
142 calories per serving

Vanilla-flavored vodka paired with the slightly spicy, slightly lemony-lime flavor of ginger ale tastes like a yummy piece of birthday cake! So you can have your cake and drink it for less than 150 calories. Use diet ginger ale and you come in under 100! **Serves 1**

1½ ounces vanilla-flavored vodka, homemade (recipe follows) or store bought

4 ounces very cold ginger ale (or diet ginger ale)

Crushed ice

Sliced strawberry or raspberries, for garnish

Combine the vodka and ginger ale in a rocks glass.

Add crushed ice, garnish with a strawberry or raspberries, and serve.

HOMEMADE VANILLA VODKA

Split 2 fresh vanilla beans lengthwise and scrape the seeds into a bottle of vodka.

Refrigerate for at least 2 days and up to 1 month.

COTTON CANDY

134 calories per serving

This cocktail is like a favorite carnival treat in a glass! However, our version has all of the flavor but virtually none of the calories and sugar. For more of a slushy consistency, make it with crushed ice. **Serves 1**

Ice

1½ ounces vanilla-flavored vodka, homemade (page 73) or store bought

1 ounce canned unsweetened pineapple juice

1 teaspoon grenadine

Vanilla club soda

Fresh pineapple wedge, for garnish (optional)

In a cup filled with ice, combine the vodka, pineapple juice, and grenadine.

Top with the club soda, garnish with a pineapple wedge, if desired, and serve.

APPLE, ELDERFLOWER & VODKA COCKTAIL

143 calories per serving

Elderflower liqueur is made from the elderflower, a small, white starry flower that blooms through the spring and summer in Germany and Austria. In Europe, the flower is used to flavor many foods and drinks, but in the United States it's gaining popularity in the form of a liqueur. The flavor is floral with undertones of citrus and fruit, like peach and pear.

Serves 1

3 ounces unfiltered apple juice

1 ounce vodka or raspberry-flavored vodka

2 teaspoons elderflower liqueur, such as St. Germain

Ice cubes

Splash of peach-, raspberry-, or orange-flavored club soda

1 thin slice Gala apple, for garnish

5 fresh raspberries, for garnish

Fresh mint sprig, for garnish

Combine the apple juice, vodka, and elderflower liqueur in a tall glass. Add ice cubes and top with club soda. Garnish with the apple slice, raspberries, and mint sprig and serve.

CHAMPAGNE FLOAT

130 calories per serving

What could be more decadent than a champagne float? This can be a perfect "dessert" cocktail, or think of it as a new spin on the mimosa. The variations are endless—try different sorbet flavors, or mixing and matching, too: mango-pineapple, raspberry-lemon, blueberry-pomegranate. Just keep the total amount of sorbet to ¼ cup (2 ounces) and the total amount of sparkling wine to 3 ounces, and you're good to go. **Serves 1**

2 ounces (¼ cup) orange sorbet

3 ounces very cold sparkling wine or champagne

Fresh mint sprig, for garnish

Put the sorbet into a white wine glass and pour the sparkling wine over the top. Garnish with the mint sprig and serve.

SPARKLING CHERRY LEMONADE

135 calories per serving

This is not the pink lemonade from your childhood made with lots of sugar and a splash of grenadine. This grown-up version is not only delicious but "pretty in pink" to look at, too. If you can't find cherry juice or you aren't a fan, a splash of cranberry juice or pomegranate juice will do nicely. **Serves 1**

½ teaspoon finely grated lemon zest

Juice of 1 lemon

2 teaspoons agave or Simple Syrup (page 11)

1 tablespoon cherry juice

Crushed ice

3 ounces very cold sparkling wine

Lemon slice, for garnish

Fresh mint sprig, for garnish

Maraschino cherry, for garnish (optional)

Combine the lemon zest and juice, simple syrup, and cherry juice in a rocks glass. Add crushed ice and the sparkling wine. Garnish with the lemon slice, mint sprig, and cherry, if using.

SUMMERY
SIPS

BLUEBERRY-GINGER FIZZY

125 calories per serving

Blueberries are high in antioxidants and low in calories. They go together beautifully with the fresh ginger and champagne in this lovely drink. Using sugar-free blueberry juice cocktail will reduce the calories to 98 per serving.

Serves 4

½ cup fresh blueberries

1 tablespoon peeled and finely grated fresh ginger

1 tablespoon agave

Juice of 1 lime

1 cup regular or sugar-free blueberry juice cocktail, such as Ocean Spray

12 ounces very cold champagne or sparkling wine

In the bottom of a pitcher, muddle the blueberries, ginger, agave, and lime juice using a wooden muddler or spoon. Stir in the blueberry juice cocktail and the champagne and serve in chilled champagne flutes.

MANGO-RUM
ICED TEA

109 calories per serving

Tea is a great calorie-free ingredient that adds lots of flavor. Make sure to purchase either the black or green varieties, not ones labeled "flavored sweetened iced tea mixes"—those contain about 80 calories a glass. **Serves 8**

7 cups water

1 tablespoon sugar

7 mango black tea bags (such as Republic of Tea)

1¼ cups dark rum

1 medium fresh ripe mango, peeled, pitted, and finely chopped

1 lime, thinly sliced

½ orange, thinly sliced

Ice cubes

In a medium saucepan, bring the 7 cups of water and the sugar to a boil. Add the tea bags, remove the pan from the heat, and let steep for 5 minutes. Discard the bags and let the tea cool to room temperature.

Transfer the cooled tea to a pitcher, add the rum, mango, and the lime and orange slices. Cover and refrigerate until the tea is cold and the flavors have melded, at least 2 hours and up to 24 hours.

To serve, pour the tea into tall glasses filled with ice cubes and garnish with fruit from the pitcher.

VARIATIONS

PASSION FRUIT–PAPAYA–RUM ICED TEA Replace the mango tea bags with passion fruit-papaya ones. Replace the mango with chopped fresh papaya.

PEACH-GINGER ICED BLACK TEA WITH BOURBON Replace the mango tea with peach-ginger black tea bags and replace the dark rum with bourbon or whiskey. Replace the mango with chopped fresh or frozen peaches.

CRANBERRY-BLOOD ORANGE ICED TEA WITH VODKA Replace the mango tea bags with cranberry–blood orange tea bags and replace the dark rum with vodka. Replace the mango with blood or regular oranges.

BAY BREEZE PUNCH

85 calories per serving

White cranberry juice adds a lovely sweetness, without the sharp bite of red cranberry, to this cocktail that's loosely based on the classic Sea Breeze. Club soda adds fizz and makes it fun! **Serves 6**

1 cup white cranberry juice

½ cup unsweetened apple juice

½ cup canned unsweetened pineapple juice

1 cup vodka

Crushed ice

Orange- or lime-flavored club soda

Pineapple slice or lime slice, for garnish

In a small pitcher, combine the cranberry, apple, and pineapple juices and the vodka. Cover and refrigerate for at least 1 hour and up to 24 hours.

Divide the punch among 6 tall glasses filled with crushed ice. Fill to the top with club soda, garnish with the pineapple or lime slice, and serve.

WATERMELON SWIZZLE

119 calories per serving

Using a slice of watermelon as a swizzle stick is fun and earth friendly, since none of the fruit will go to waste—and it even adds a little flavor! The rum gives this drink a very tropical feel, but a flavored vodka would work equally well. **Serves 1**

½ lime, cut in half

3 fresh mint leaves

½ cup finely chopped fresh watermelon

1½ ounces white rum

Club soda

1-inch-wide x 4-inch-long stick of watermelon, rind on, for garnish (optional)

Fresh mint sprig, for garnish (optional)

In a tall glass, muddle the lime, mint leaves, and ¼ cup of the watermelon.

Add the rum, the remaining ¼ cup of watermelon, and fill to top with club soda. Garnish with a watermelon swizzle stick and mint sprig, if desired, and serve.

BASIL-CUCUMBER COOLER

119 calories per serving

This cocktail looks like it jumped right off a spa cuisine menu—and it is low enough in calories to be qualified to appear on one. **Serves 1**

2-inch piece of cucumber, peeled and chopped

1 teaspoon grated lemon zest

2 leaves fresh basil

1 teaspoon agave

1½ ounces gin

2 tablespoons fresh lemon juice

Ice cubes

Splash of lemon-flavored seltzer water

1 thin slice lemon, for garnish

1 thin slice or spear of English cucumber, for garnish

In a cocktail shaker, muddle the chopped cucumber, lemon zest, basil, and agave.

Add the gin, lemon juice, and ice cubes and stir for 10 seconds. Strain the mixture into a rocks glass filled with ice cubes and top with seltzer. Garnish with the lemon and cucumber slices and serve.

VARIATION

SAGE-, DILL-, OR MINT-CUCUMBER COOLER Substitute fresh sage, dill, or mint for the basil.

RASPBERRY-LEMON COOLER

127 calories per serving
(with diet soda: 92)

There is something magical about the combination of sweet, vibrant-red raspberries and tart, pale-yellow lemon, whether in desserts or in fun cocktails like this one. Raspberries are a rich source of vitamins and minerals and have a host of health benefits. Using red-berry vodka or lemon vodka will intensify the flavor even more. **Serves 4**

1 cup fresh ripe raspberries

1 tablespoon sugar or agave

Grated zest and juice of 1 lemon

4 ounces lemon- or red berry–flavored vodka, or plain vodka

Crushed ice

1½ cups cold lemon-lime soda or diet lemon-lime soda, or regular or diet or lemon-flavored seltzer

In a small bowl, combine ¾ cup of the raspberries, the sugar, and the lemon zest and juice. Let sit at room temperature for 15 minutes, then mash the berries with a fork.

Put the remaining ¼ cup of raspberries on a plate and put in the freezer until frozen, at least 1 hour and up to 24 hours.

Fill 4 tall glasses with ice, divide the raspberry syrup and vodka among the glasses, and fill to the top with soda. Garnish with the frozen raspberries and serve.

BLUEBERRY LEMONADE

143 calories per serving
(with diet lemonade: 101)

The combination of blueberries and lemon is a match made in cocktail heaven. Blueberry-flavored vodka is a great way to get flavor without calories—and feel free to experiment by swapping in a different fruit-flavored vodka, such as raspberry, grapefruit, or mango. **Serves 1**

1½ ounces cold blueberry vodka

3 ounces cold lemonade, regular or low-calorie (such as Newman's Own Organic Virgin Lemonade or Diet Virgin Lemonade)

2 thin slices lemon

5 fresh blueberries, frozen

In a rocks glass, stir together the vodka and lemonade. Add the lemon slices and frozen berries and serve.

FESTIVE
DRINKS

SPICY APPLE

131 calories per serving

Ginger beer isn't actually beer at all, but rather a nonalcoholic carbonated soft drink. You can drink it on its own (it's very similar to ginger ale) or use it as a mixer in cocktails. It's rarely available as a diet variety, but you can substitute a really good-quality diet ginger ale if you prefer to reduce the total amount of calories. **Serves 1**

1 ounce vanilla-flavored vodka, homemade (page 73) or store bought

3 ounces cold apple cider

2 ounces ginger beer

Ice cubes

1 cinnamon stick, for garnish

3 thin slices Gala or Fuji apple, for garnish

In a rocks glass, combine the vodka, cider, and ginger beer. Add ice cubes, garnish with the cinnamon stick and apple slices, and serve.

EGGNOG

135 calories per serving

A serving of traditional eggnog—made with lots of egg yolks, whole milk, heavy cream, and a heavy dose of bourbon, brandy, or rum—contains about 350 calories and a gut-busting 19 grams of fat. Bah! Humbug! This version, which is every bit as flavorful and creamy, contains only 135 calories per serving. **Serves 6**

2½ **cups cold 1% milk**

1 **vanilla bean**

1 **cinnamon stick**

2 **large eggs**

3 **tablespoons sugar**

1 **teaspoon cornstarch**

¼ **cup cold spiced rum or bourbon**

Freshly grated nutmeg, for garnish

Fat-free whipped cream, for garnish (optional)

In a medium saucepan set over low heat, heat 2 cups of the milk. Split the vanilla bean lengthwise, scrape the seeds into the pan, and put the pod in the pan, too. Add the cinnamon stick and heat the milk until simmering, about 5 minutes.

Remove the pan from the heat and let the mixture steep for 15 minutes. Return the pan to low heat and bring the mixture back to a simmer.

In a large bowl, whisk the eggs, sugar, and cornstarch together until the egg mixture thickens and becomes pale, about 2 minutes.

(recipe continues)

Remove the cinnamon stick and vanilla pod from the milk, and then slowly whisk the hot milk into the egg mixture.

Return the mixture to the pan, set the pan over low heat, and cook, stirring constantly with a wooden spoon, until the mixture thickens and coats the back of the wooden spoon, about 5 minutes.

Remove the pan from the heat and immediately stir in the remaining ½ cup of cold milk and the cold rum to cool down the mixture.

Transfer the eggnog to a pitcher or bowl, cover, and refrigerate until very cold, at least 1 hour and up to 24 hours.

To serve, pour the eggnog into 6 cups and garnish with the nutmeg and whipped cream, if desired.

VARIATION

CHOCOLATE-CINNAMON-ORANGE EGGNOG In step 1, add 2 tablespoons of natural cocoa powder and a 2-inch piece of orange peel to the 2 cups of milk. Replace the grated nutmeg with ground cinnamon. Top with whipped cream and garnish with a cinnamon stick. (calories: 139)

HOT TODDY

75 calories per serving

It seems too good to be true! A warm, satisfying, sweet, boozy mug of goodness with only 75 calories a serving. Feel free to add any spices that you like, or even a few tea bags to add depth of flavor without additional calories. **Serves 6**

4 cups water

2 cinnamon sticks

3 cloves

1 star anise

3-inch strip of orange zest

2-inch strip of lemon zest

3 tablespoons honey or agave

¼ cup bourbon, brandy, or dark rum

In a medium saucepan set over high heat, combine the water, cinnamon sticks, cloves, star anise, and the orange and lemon zests. Bring to boil, turn off the heat, cover, and let steep for 30 minutes.

Bring back to a simmer, add the honey and bourbon, and cook for 2 minutes. Pour into 6 heatproof mugs and serve.

HOT BUTTERED BOURBON

120 calories per serving

Most people are familiar with hot buttered rum, but there is something very southern and comforting about using bourbon in this dessert-like drink. **Serves 6**

2 tablespoon unsalted butter

2 tablespoons dark brown sugar

6 ounces bourbon

2 cups apple cider

2 cups hot water

1 recipe mulling spices (recipe follows)

1 small orange, quartered

1 small lemon, halved

Cinnamon sticks, for garnish

In a medium saucepan set over medium heat, melt the butter. Cook until it turns light golden brown, about 2 minutes. Whisk in the sugar and cook until the sugar has dissolved, about 4 minutes.

Add the bourbon and cook until reduced by half, about 5 minutes.

Add the cider, water, mulling spices, orange, and lemon. Reduce the heat to low and simmer for 15 minutes. Remove the pot from the heat, cover, and let steep for another 15 minutes.

Remove the mulling spices and orange and lemon. Return the pan to low heat and bring to a simmer.

Ladle into heatproof mugs, garnish with a cinnamon stick, and serve.

HOMEMADE MULLING SPICES

Put 2 cinnamon sticks, 8 whole cloves, 4 allspice berries, and a pinch of grated nutmeg into a square of cheesecloth. Tie the cloth closed with kitchen twine.

GINGER-PEAR NIGHTCAP

131 calories per serving

The combination of ginger and pears is classic in the dessert world. Kick back, put your feet up, and sip it slowly for a perfect way to end your day. **Serves 1**

Ice cubes

2 teaspoons Fresh Ginger Simple Syrup (page 11)

2 ounces cold pear nectar

1 ounce cognac or brandy

1 fresh twist of orange, for garnish

In a cocktail shaker filled with ice cubes, combine the simple syrup, pear nectar, and cognac. Shake for 10 seconds.

Strain into a brandy snifter, garnish with the twist of orange, and serve.

VANILLA-CHAMOMILE HOT TODDY

97 calories per serving

Hot toddys are the perfect drink on a cold winter night. Chamomile has been imbibed for centuries and offers many health benefits, including soothing stomachaches and promoting sleep. You can also refrigerate this mixture and serve it over ice on a hot summer's day. **Serves 4**

4 cups water

4 chamomile tea bags

2 tablespoons honey

1 vanilla bean, split

2 orange slices, plus 4 more for garnish

4 ounces white rum

In a medium saucepan, bring 4 cups of water to a boil. Add the tea bags, honey, vanilla bean, and 2 of the orange slices. Remove the pan from the heat, cover, and steep for 10 minutes.

Strain the mixture, discarding the solids, and return the tea to the pan. Heat on low, and bring to a simmer.

Divide the tea among 4 heatproof mugs and add 1 ounce of the rum to each. Garnish each with the remaining orange slices and serve.

HOT TEA-TO

150 calories per serving

This mash-up of a hot toddy and a mojito is perfect for drinking on a cold winter's night when you are dreaming about being on a hot sandy beach. The combination of tea and mint is always a winner—add rum, and . . . jackpot! If you can find pure cane sugar, use it, as its natural molasses flavor makes this drink much more complex and very reminiscent of the Islands. **Serves 2**

2 cups water

2 black tea bags

¼ cup packed fresh mint leaves

2 tablespoons pure cane sugar

2 ounces dark rum

In a small saucepan set over high heat, bring 2 cups of water to a boil. Add the tea bags, mint, and sugar, remove the pan from the heat, and cover. Let steep for 5 minutes.

Remove the tea bags, strain into 2 heatproof mugs, and add the rum. Serve hot.

CIDER PUNCH

**140 calories per serving
(with diet ginger ale: 119)**

This punch, full of fall flavors and ingredients, would be perfect served at a Halloween party or after a day of apple picking. **Serves 6**

2 cups sparkling cider

6 ounces brandy

1 small orange, halved and thinly sliced

1½ cups regular or diet dry ginger ale

1 small Granny Smith apple, cored, halved, thinly sliced, and put in the freezer

In a pitcher, combine the cider, brandy, and orange slices. Cover and refrigerate for at least 1 hour and up to 4 hours.

Remove the orange slices from the pitcher and set aside. Divide the mixture among 6 punch glasses or champagne flutes and top with a splash of ginger ale.

To serve, garnish with a few frozen apple slices and a reserved orange slice, if desired.

DESSERT
COCKTAILS

CREAMY BANANA DAIQUIRI

150 calories per serving

This tropical concoction with a just a touch of fizz will make you feel like you are on an island vacation even if you are in your own backyard. **Serves 2**

2 ounces dark or white rum

1 frozen medium banana, peeled and chopped

1 teaspoon freshly grated lime zest

Juice of 1 lime

4 frozen Vanilla "Creamy" Cubes (page 102)

½ cup lime-flavored seltzer or club soda

2 lime wedges, for garnish

In a blender, combine the rum, banana, lime zest and juice, creamy cubes, and seltzer water and blend until smooth.

Divide between 2 rocks glasses, garnish each with a lime wedge, and serve.

"CREAMY" CUBES
14 calories per cube

"Creamy" is in quotation marks because we all know that cream and low-calorie do not mix. Here is a way to add a creamy look and feel to cocktails that ordinarily call for cream, coconut milk, or full-fat milk. **Makes 16 cubes**

2 cups Skim Plus milk

2 tablespoon Simple Syrup (page 11) or agave

1 standard ice cube tray

In a glass measuring cup, whisk together the milk and the simple syrup. Pour the mixture into the ice cube tray and freeze until frozen, at least 2 hours.

VARIATIONS

CHOCOLATE "CREAMY" CUBES Replace regular Skim Plus milk with Chocolate Skim Plus milk and omit the simple syrup. (calories per cube: 20)

PEPPERMINT OR PEPPERMINT-CHOCOLATE "CREAMY" CUBES Add ½ teaspoon pure peppermint extract to either the plain recipe or the chocolate variety.

VANILLA "CREAMY" CUBES Add 1 teaspoon pure vanilla extract to the plain recipe.

HAZELNUT "CREAMY" CUBES Add ¼ teaspoon pure hazelnut extract to the plain recipe.

ORANGE OR ORANGE-CHOCOLATE "CREAMY" CUBES Add ¼ teaspoon pure orange extract to the plain or chocolate recipes.

COCONUT OR CHOCOLATE-COCONUT "CREAMY" CUBES Add 1 teaspoon pure coconut extract to the plain or chocolate.

COCONUT-RUM-BANANA SPRITZER

149 calories per serving
(using club soda: 99)

A piña colada without any of the guilt! Just as in the Creamy Banana Daiquiri (page 101), the addition of frozen milk and a frozen banana makes for a rich, creamy consistency without any excess fat or calories. Champagne gives a lovely finish to this dessert-like cocktail, but to save even more calories, use a lime-flavored club soda instead. **Serves 6**

16 frozen Vanilla "Creamy" Cubes (page 102)

2 tablespoons Skim Plus milk

1 medium banana, frozen, peeled, and quartered

¼ cup coconut rum

1½ cups chilled champagne or sparkling wine, or lime-flavored club soda

In a blender, combine the "creamy" cubes, milk, banana, and rum and blend until smooth.

Divide among 6 rocks glasses or champagne flutes, top with champagne, and serve.

COFFEE MILK PUNCH

147 calories per serving

This New Orleans classic can be served in a punch bowl or straight up in a frosted glass. The original version is traditionally decadent, made with cups of bourbon, chicory, whole milk, heavy cream, and sugar. Our version has all the flavors of the original with about one-fifth the calories and none of the fat! **Serves 1**

1 ounce bourbon

2 teaspoons Simple Syrup (page 11)

⅛ teaspoon vanilla extract

⅓ cup Skim Plus or skim milk

1½ ounces chilled espresso

4 ice cubes

Dash of nutmeg

Put a rocks glass in the freezer for 10 minutes.

In a cocktail shaker, combine the bourbon, simple syrup, vanilla, milk, espresso, and 4 ice cubes. Shake vigorously for 10 seconds, until very frothy and cold.

Strain into the cold rocks glass, top with the nutmeg, and serve.

GRASSHOPPER

145 calories per serving

A bright-green mint-flavored cocktail, the grasshopper is originally from a bar in New Orleans' French Quarter. This vodka version (often known as a vodka grasshopper or flying grasshopper) is considerably less caloric and less green in color—but still does the trick! **Serves 4**

16 frozen Peppermint "Creamy" Cubes (page 102)

½ cup Skim Plus milk or skim milk

4 ounces vodka

1 tablespoon finely grated bittersweet chocolate (60% cacao)

In a blender, combine the "creamy" cubes, milk, and vodka and blend until smooth. Add the chocolate and pulse a few times to incorporate. Divide among 4 rocks glasses and serve.

VARIATION

DOUBLE CHOCOLATE GRASSHOPPER Substitute peppermint-chocolate "creamy" cubes (page 102) in place of the peppermint "creamy" cubes. (calories: 135)

HAZELNUT BOURBON "CREAM"

146 calories per serving

The combination of hazelnuts and bourbon may seem odd, but they actually have a natural affinity for each other. This cocktail takes those flavors and turns them into a dessert-worthy low-calorie drink. **Serves 4**

16 frozen Hazelnut "Creamy" Cubes (page 102)
½ cup skim milk
4 ounces bourbon
2 tablespoons Reddi-wip

In a blender, combine the "creamy" cubes, milk, and bourbon and blend until smooth.

Divide among 4 rocks glasses, top each with a small squirt of the Reddi-wip, and serve.

MANGO-ORANGE CRUSH

150 calories per serving

A version of your favorite orange soda from childhood—but with a kick! Orange and lime juice and zest are a nice match for mango, which is the star of this cocktail. **Serves 1**

½ cup fresh or frozen mango chunks

1 teaspoon grated orange zest

1 teaspoon grated lime zest

Juice of 1 lime

1½ ounces orange-flavored vodka

Crushed ice

Orange-flavored club soda or seltzer

In a blender, combine the mango, orange and lime zests, lime juice, and vodka and blend until smooth.

Pour the mixture into a tall glass filled with crushed ice, top off with the orange soda, and serve.

FROZEN CANTALOUPE & PEACH TEA DAIQUIRI

133 calories per serving

Using tea in cocktails is a healthy and fun way to add flavor without calories. The combination of peach tea with cantaloupe is delicious, and freezing the fruit is a great way to add creaminess to the cocktail without lots of extra calories and fat tagging along. **Serves 1**

½ cup water

1 peach tea bag

1½ ounces melon-flavored vodka, such as Van Gogh, or regular vodka

½ cup cubed and frozen fresh cantaloupe

1 tablespoon fresh lemon juice

Lemon or orange club soda (optional)

In a small saucepan, bring the water to a boil. Add the peach tea bag, remove the pan from the heat, and let steep for 5 minutes. Remove the tea bag and put the tea in the freezer until cold, about 10 minutes.

In a blender, combine the cold tea, vodka, cantaloupe, and lemon juice and blend until smooth. Serve in tall glass, topped with a splash of soda water, if desired.

BOURBON PEACH FUZZ

113 calories per serving

Nothing says southern like bourbon and peaches. This cocktail is chock-full of both! Think of this blush-colored drink as an adults-only smoothie. A splash of orange club soda adds a bit of lightness and additional citrus flavor without the calories. **Serves 4**

1 cup frozen Vanilla "Creamy" Cubes (page 102)

1 cup frozen peaches, partially thawed

¼ cup fresh orange juice

3 ounces bourbon

Splash of orange-flavored club soda (optional)

4 orange wedges, for garnish

In a blender, combine the milk, "creamy" cubes, peaches, orange juice, and bourbon. Blend until smooth.

Divide among 4 glasses and top with a splash of orange club soda, if desired. Garnish each glass with an orange wedge and serve.

VEGAN MUDSLIDE

132 calories per serving

Almond milk is a delicious alternative to cow's milk that even nonvegans will love. This cocktail tastes like one of those pricey, high-calorie concoctions from trendy coffee shops, but it has many, many fewer calories. The crushed ice makes it an adults-only snow cone! **Serves 1**

4 ounces strong brewed coffee or espresso

3 ounces almond milk

1½ ounces vanilla-flavored vodka, homemade (page 73) or store bought

Crushed ice

Combine the coffee, almond milk, and vodka in a tall glass. Fill the glass with crushed ice and serve.

VARIATION

MOCHA MUDSLIDE Substitute chocolate- or mocha-flavored almond milk for plain almond milk.

SKINNY
SNACKS

RED CHILE–LIME ROASTED CHICKPEAS

110 calories per serving

Long a staple of Middle Eastern and Italian cuisine, the chickpea (garbanzo bean) has recently become a pantry staple in the United States, thanks to the sudden popularity of hummus. Very low in calories and high in protein, chickpeas make an excellent healthy snack that goes perfectly with a cocktail. **Serves 8**

2 (15-ounce) cans of chickpeas, rinsed and drained

1½ tablespoons olive or canola oil

Finely grated zest of 1 lime

Juice of 1 lime

1 teaspoon chile powder

¼ teaspoon ground cumin

1 teaspoon kosher salt, plus more to taste

Preheat the oven to 400°F.

In a medium bowl, combine the chickpeas, oil, lime zest, half the lime juice, plus the chile powder, cumin, and 1 teaspoon of salt. Spread the chickpeas in an even layer on a baking sheet.

Bake, shaking the pan every 10 minutes, until lightly golden brown and crisp, about 35 minutes.

Remove the pan from the oven and sprinkle the remaining lime juice on the chickpeas. Season to taste with salt, and serve.

BLACK PEPPER–PARMESAN HOT-AIR-POPPED POPCORN

85 calories per 2-cup serving

Using a spray bottle for your oil is a great way to control the amount. A Misto brand sprayer creates a fine mist, but a simple plastic spray bottle from the hardware store works nicely, too. **Makes 16 cups; serves 8**

½ cup popcorn kernels

Olive oil spray

3 tablespoons grated Parmigiano Reggiano

1 teaspoon kosher salt

½ teaspoon freshly ground black pepper

Pop the corn in a hot-air popper according to the manufacturer's directions. (Or put 2 tablespoons of popcorn kernels in a paper lunch bag. Fold the top of the bag over and tape it down. Microwave for about 1 minute and 30 seconds. Repeat with the remaining kernels.)

Transfer the popped corn to a large bowl and spray with about 1 tablespoon of olive oil spray. Add the Parmesan, salt, and pepper and toss to combine. Serve immediately.

VARIATION

BUFFALO-PARMESAN HOT-AIR-POPPED POPCORN Substitute 2 tablespoons melted unsalted butter for the olive oil spray and add 2 tablespoons Tabasco and ¼ teaspoon chile powder. Decrease the cheese to 2 tablespoons. (calories per serving: 107)

SESAME KALE CHIPS

110 calories per serving

Kale is on just about every restaurant menu and in everything from soups to salads, omelets, and pasta—with good reason. This leafy green is a superhero of the vegetable world. It's packed with calcium and iron, plus vitamins A, C, and K, and only has 15 calories per ounce.
These simple kale chips will have you tossing aside your favorite potato variety in no time flat. **Serves 4**

1 tablespoon olive oil

2 teaspoons low-sodium soy or tamari sauce

1 tablespoon fresh lemon juice

1 large bunch kale (10 ounces), stems and ribs removed and leaves torn

2 teaspoons sesame seeds

Preheat oven to 325°F.

In a small bowl, whisk together the oil, soy sauce, and lemon juice and transfer the mixture to a Misto or spray bottle.

Lay the kale out on a large baking sheet. Spray the tops with the oil mixture and sprinkle with the sesame seeds.

Bake until crisp, about 15 minutes.

VARIATION

SEA SALT & BLACK PEPPER KALE CHIPS Omit the soy sauce, lemon juice, and sesame seeds. Spray the kale with oil and season with sea salt and freshly ground black pepper.

BEET CHIPS
WITH GOAT CHEESE DIP
75 calories per serving

The earthy flavor of beets, the tangy flavor of goat cheese, and the sweetness of balsamic dressing have been popular for years at trendy restaurants. This variation gives that classic combination a new form and fewer calories. **Serves 8**

2 medium beets

Olive oil spray

Salt and freshly ground black pepper

Goat Cheese Dip (recipe follows)

Preheat the oven to 325°F. Place the oven racks in the lower and upper third of the oven. Spray two baking sheets with olive oil.

Peel the beets with a vegetable peeler and, using either a mandolin or a sharp knife, slice them 1/16 inch thick.

Divide the beet slices between the baking sheets, spray the tops of the beets with olive oil, and season with salt and pepper.

Bake for 20 minutes, then rotate the baking sheets between the oven racks. Bake until the chips are crispy, 15 to 25 more minutes, depending on your oven and how thinly you sliced the beets. Remove the pans from the oven and let cool for 10 minutes.

Transfer the chips to a wire rack to keep them crispy. Serve warm or at room temperature with the Goat Cheese Dip (recipe follows) on the side.

GOAT CHEESE DIP

makes 1½ cups

1 cup fat-free plain Greek yogurt

2 teaspoons balsamic vinegar

4 ounces herb-and-garlic goat cheese spread

Kosher salt and freshly ground black pepper

In a small bowl, whisk together the yogurt, vinegar, and goat cheese. Season with salt and pepper to taste.

Store the dip in an airtight container in the refrigerator for 1 day.

ARTICHOKE VERDI CROSTINI

58 calories per serving

Crostini are the perfect bar snack and can be topped with just about anything. This lovely green-hued herbaceous version pays homage to the healthy ingredients and flavors of the Mediterranean. **Makes 24; serves 8**

1 (14-ounce) can of artichoke hearts in water, drained

12 green pitted olives, such as Picholine

1 large garlic clove, coarsely chopped

1 tablespoon capers, drained

Grated zest and juice of ½ lemon

3 tablespoons fresh flat-leaf parsley leaves, plus more for garnish

2 tablespoons chopped fresh mint

Kosher salt and freshly ground black pepper

24 whole grain crackers, such as Kashi

In the bowl of a food processor, combine the artichokes, olives, garlic, capers, lemon zest and juice, and a splash of cold water. Process until smooth and creamy. Add the parsley, mint, and salt and pepper to taste and pulse until incorporated.

Divide the artichoke mixture among the crackers and serve on a platter. Garnish with more chopped herbs, if desired.

SMOKED SALMON & CUCUMBER ROLLS

41 calories per serving

Smoked salmon is rich and salty and fatty—all the things that we crave when drinking a cocktail. But because of this, a small amount can be very satisfying. Cucumber and mustard add the perfect crunch and a bit of sweet heat. **Makes 24; serves 8**

¼ **cup Dijon mustard**

1 teaspoon honey

Freshly ground black pepper

24 paper-thin slices of smoked salmon (about 7 ounces)

½ **English cucumber, seeded and julienned**

2 tablespoons finely chopped fresh dill

In a small bowl, whisk together the mustard, honey, and pepper.

Spread the salmon slices out on a flat work surface and brush them with the mustard mixture. Put a small bunch of cucumbers in the center of each slice and roll up securely.

Arrange the rolls on a platter, seam side down, and sprinkle with the dill. Serve cold.

ROASTED OLIVES
WITH GREEN CHILE & MINT
66 calories per serving

Roasting olives is an unexpected technique that will surprise and intrigue your guests. The salty-spicy flavor of the naturally low-calorie olives makes them the perfect low-calorie bar food. **Serves 8**

3 cups mixed green and black pitted olives

2 teaspoons olive oil

1 jalapeño, thinly sliced

Kosher salt and freshly ground black pepper

2 tablespoons finely chopped fresh mint

Preheat the oven to 350°F.

In a small baking dish, combine the olives, oil, and jalapeño and season with a touch of salt and pepper. Cover with foil and roast until heated through, about 15 minutes.

Transfer the olives to a bowl, stir in the mint, and serve.

VARIATION

ROASTED OLIVES WITH RED CHILE & CILANTRO Substitute ⅛ teaspoon of red chile flakes for the jalapeño and cilantro for the mint.

GREEK SALAD SKEWERS

107 calories per serving

A classic Greek salad together in one perfect mouthful.
Substitute mozzarella for the feta, fresh basil for the dill,
and red wine vinegar for balsamic, and you have the classic
Caprese salad. **Serves 8**

½ cup balsamic vinegar

1 tablespoon fresh lemon
juice

1 teaspoon extra-virgin
olive oil

Kosher salt and freshly
ground black pepper

6-inch skewers

32 cherry tomatoes

8-ounce block of feta,
drained on paper towels
and cut into 16 cubes

2 tablespoons finely
chopped fresh dill

In a small saucepan set over medium heat, bring the vinegar to a
simmer and cook until it has reduced by half, about 5 minutes. Let
cool to room temperature, whisk in the lemon juice and olive oil and
season with salt and pepper to taste.

To assemble the salad, on each skewer place a cherry tomato,
followed by a cube of feta and an additional cherry tomato.
Drizzle the skewers with the balsamic glaze and sprinkle with the
chopped dill.

VARIATION

CAPRESE SALAD SKEWERS Substitute 16 small balls of mozzarella
for the feta and 16 basil leaves for the dill (calories per serving: 88).

EASY TANDOORI CHICKEN LETTUCE WRAPS

89 calories per serving

Tandoori flavor in less than 15 minutes, and healthy, too? You bet. Be sure to buy ground chicken made with white meat, which is much lower in calories and fat than dark meat. You can also substitute ground turkey breast and use raspberry or peach vinaigrette. **Makes 16; serves 8**

1 tablespoon canola oil

1 small Spanish onion, finely chopped

2 garlic cloves, finely chopped

1½ tablespoons mild curry powder

¼ cup fat-free plain Greek yogurt, at room temperature

Nonstick cooking spray

1 pound ground lean chicken

Kosher salt and freshly ground black pepper

Few dashes of hot-pepper sauce

2 green onions, green and pale green parts, thinly sliced

16 Bibb lettuce leaves

Mango Chutney Vinaigrette (recipe follows)

In a medium nonstick sauté pan set over medium heat, heat the oil. Add the onion and cook until soft, about 4 minutes. Add the garlic and cook for 1 minute. Stir in the curry powder and cook for 1 minute. Add 1 cup of water and cook until the mixture thickens and becomes a paste, about 5 minutes. Remove the pan from the heat and let cool for 5 minutes.

Transfer the mixture to a bowl and stir in the yogurt.

Return the pan to high heat and spray it with nonstick cooking spray. Add the chicken and salt and pepper to taste and cook, stirring occasionally, until the chicken is golden brown and cooked through, about 8 minutes.

Transfer the chicken to the yogurt mixture, add the green onions, and stir well.

Arrange the lettuce on a platter and drizzle with some of the vinaigrette. Spoon the chicken mixture into the leaves and serve warm.

MANGO CHUTNEY VINAIGRETTE
makes about ½ cup

2 tablespoons prepared mango chutney

Juice of 1 lime

2 tablespoons red or white wine vinegar

1 tablespoon finely chopped fresh mint

Salt and freshly ground black pepper

In a small bowl, whisk together the chutney, lime, vinegar, and mint and season with salt and pepper to taste.

Store in an airtight container in the refrigerator for 5 days.

INDEX